THE DRAWINGS

OF EDGAR

DEGAS

DRAWINGS

EDGAR

DEGAS

BY

PROFESSOR JAROMÍR PEČÍRKA

Peter Nevill • London

Graphic design by Z. Sklenář

Translated by Ivo A. Havlů

Designed and a produced by Artia for

Peter Nevill

Westbook House • Fulham Broadway • London

© 1963 by Artia

Printed in Czechoslovakia

s 1447

Contents

'*Works of art must not resemble chance.*'
'*A drawing alone is not a form, it is an
experience of a form.*'
(From Degas' aphorisms)

I The Misanthrope

Edgar Degas was said to be a pessimist who anxiously concealed himself within the shell of his privacy. He was known to be an irritable person, some even went so far as to speak of him as a wicked man. Others claimed he did not like people, that he had a fancy for cruel jokes and would not be afraid to use words which might hurt someone else's feelings. On one occasion when a journalist sought to interview him, Degas answered, 'What business of yours is it whether I choose to make paintings, shoes or stockings? That is my private life, sir!' An artistic creation considered to be one's private life! Delacroix would not be alone in agreeing with this definition. It would be in accordance with all the artists of the 19th and 20th centuries who expressed their relation to the world through their work; whose lives and art merged together forming a single inseparable truth. Let us, then, look for the truth of Degas' character in his works.

Degas' paintings and drawings quite clearly reveal that his relation towards mankind was not one of disinterest, or indifference. Meier-Graefe had his doubts about the much emphasised heartlessness and inhumanity of Degas, by asking, 'Was Degas heartless? He was said to be. Which may have been caused by the abundance of emotion that made Degas incapable of showing his feelings. Perhaps he loved so fanatically that in the end hatred was the product of his excessive enthusiasm.'[1] An eye-witness, Ambroise Vollard, once wrote that Degas' hatred towards women was generally assumed. 'However, nobody loved women more than he, but it was a form of bashfulness mixed with a little fear, that made him avoid women.'[2] Daniel Halévy, whose father, Ludovic, was a devoted friend of the painter produced evidence even more reliable and significant of Degas' relationship to mankind.[3] In the preface of the new edition of Degas' letters, we read the following sentences about him: [4] 'A friend he was, and that without a doubt. In order to attend a funeral, only to be able to shake hands and pay his respects, Degas travelled fifteen hours by train. All this was hidden under the mask of heartlessness, under the surface of his unusual rude manner, but it was not deeply hidden.' 'My heart is breaking,' he once wrote to a friend who was unhappy. But promptly his usual mask was put on again. 'Do you know what I have heard?' he said, storming into the home of his good friend. 'You have been telling everybody that I am not wicked at all, that people misunderstand me! What will I be left with if you take this away from me?' In addition to these testimonies let us hear what Degas has to say about himself: 'If I did not treat people the way I do (harshly), I would not be able to devote a single minute to my work. But I am timid by nature; I must always force myself to act this way (harshly).'—'People who pass their lives finding sufficient satisfaction in studying themselves alone are unhappy.'—'I frequently lock myself in my studio, I do not often see the people I love and in the end I shall suffer for it.'

My own conception of Edgar Degas which I have deduced from his letters, from passages written by his friends, but primarily from his paintings, sculptures and drawings, is far different from the deep-rooted opinion which shortly and sharply culminates by stating that cruelty is an attribute of this artist. He was never in love as a youth—he never had any youth according to Meier-Graefe. He did not become tolerant with age. There was a great deal of austerity, mathematics and visual keenness in his character as well as in his art, but he was not an irritable, obstinate man, neither was he locked up in a glass tower of deliberate solitude. On the contrary, Degas belongs to Paris like Daumier. Degas himself, as well as his works, depicts some of the most characteristic features of Paris. His paintings and drawings express and have preserved for the future some of the most effective and truthful traits of Paris during that epoch. Degas and his work are quite up to date. His art is not superficial. It would have been impossible for him to give an account of life in such an excellent, such a sad and true manner, if he were not inspired by a deep devotion for life.

II His Life

Edgar Hilaire Germain Degas, born on the 19th of June, 1834, was a descendant of an old French family. His grandfather Hilaire de Gas was an employee of the Paris stock-exchange. In the year 1793 he left for Italy where he married in Naples a girl from Genoa. He was rich, he was a banker. His son Auguste, born in Naples, moved to Paris where he opened a branch office of his father's bank, and there he married Celestine Musson, an American of French origin, whose family lived in New Orleans. Edgar was their eldest son. From the year 1870 he spelled his name Degas. As a lad he attended the Louis-le-Grand Lyceum in Paris. He was an excellent student. He was especially interested in literature. After finishing the lyceum, he studied law, upon the wish of his parents, but he found the arts more appealing. In the year 1855 he registered at the École des Beaux-Arts, but he visited the Louvre and the studio of Louis Lamoth, a painter, more frequently than school. It was Louis Lamoth who implanted in him an admiration for the art of Ingres. Thus the first strong impulse took root in Degas' aesthetic knowledge. In the year 1856, at the age of twenty-one, Degas visited Italy. He had relatives in Florence and in Naples. He remained in Italy with the exception of a number of temporary visits to Paris until 1860. He painted portraits of his relatives. He studied Signorelli's frescoes in Orvieto and Gozzoli's frescoes in Pisa. Furthermore, he became acquainted with the works of Ucello, Leonardo, Raphael, Michelangelo and other Italian masters of the Renaissance. I do not know which of these works attracted Degas most. But I would like to add, even though literature makes no mention of it, that the murals of Herculaneum and Pompeii belong to the deeper artistic impressions he experienced, because something of their softness and lightness can be detected in his paintings and drawings. But on the whole this long stay and his later visits to Italy did not leave any other profound traces in Degas' art. Jean Dominique Ingres, whose footsteps he followed in Italy, was influenced by those observations throughout his whole life. Camille Corot returned willingly to his Roman dream in the pictures of his sweet landscapes. But for Degas it seemed that he had never been there. As an old man, Degas confirmed this in a letter to A. Rouart, dated March 11, 1910: 'I no longer belong to those artists who keep running to Italy. I shall remain in my damp corner facing the Bal Tabarin.' In his time this was a generally accepted viewpoint. Rome, the aim of artists in the era of classicism, already began to lose its power of attraction in the period of Romantism. 'Rome is no longer Rome,' is what Eugène Delacroix wrote from Tangier while experiencing his Roman vision among the natives, whose white burnouses he perceived as senatorial togas. In Degas' time it was the voice of life that the artists heard calling and not the sounds of the past, and that call was so strong that they tried to give their art the features as well as the language of this life; it was their aim to characterise their art by its rhythm, colours and movements.

Upon his return to Paris, Degas went to the Louvre, where he drew the statue of the goddess Nike of Samothrace, and Mantegna's 'The Crucifixion'. He was stimulated to follow the example of Ingres, and he painted Holbein's portrait of Anne of Cleves, and Poussin's 'The Rape of the Sabines'. He worked fervently for six months on the latter canvas, taking great pains to imitate in detail Poussin's artistic methods and style. He was impressed by the violent movements and by the unusual poses of the Roman soldiers and of the abducted Sabines, without knowing then that he would, in the future, liberate human movements and poses from all such affection, pathos and theatricalism. He came to Poussin following Ingres, and perhaps also in order to anchor his own painting more firmly in the French tradition. In the early sixties under Poussin's influence, Degas painted historical themes like 'Spartan Girls Challenging the Boys' (1860), 'Semiramis Building Babylon' (1861), 'Alexander and Bucephalus'. These paintings (I have in my mind's eye the Spartan boys and girls) show a new, yet timid and reserved interest awakened in the nude body, in its movements and expressions. These paintings with the historical themes, which led Degas in the wrong direction, depict a reflection of classicism lacking in warmth. This element (thanks to Poussin's work) sank deeply into the complicated artistic consciousness of Degas. 'Poussin's spirit remained Degas' unfulfilled desire all his life long. He is indebted to Poussin for the cool mistrust with which he followed the developing trend of modern art in painting.'[5] 'I yearn for things done well, for things made with absolute precision in Poussin's style.' (Excerpt from a letter to H. Rouart; dated December 5, 1872 in New Orleans).

In the year 1863, Degas met Edouard Manet, through whose influence he stopped painting historical themes, and so realised and discovered for himself the contemporary life of Paris. From 1866 Degas belongs to his time, that is how Meier-Graefe expressed it briefly. During the war against Germany (1870—1871) he served in the infantry and later in the artillery. The commander of his unit was Henri Rouart, an engineer, a collector of modern art and Degas' school-mate and friend throughout his life. In the year 1872 Degas, accompanied by his younger brother René, journeyed to New York and from there he travelled to the birth-place of his mother, New Orleans. Degas' uncle was the manager of a huge cotton factory which belonged to the family. 'Everything here attracts me,' is what Degas wrote to a Danish painter L. Frölich on November 27, 1872, from New Orleans. 'Best of all I like the negro women of all different shades, with the little, so very white, children in their arms lingering in front of the white houses with the wooden grooved pillars, or in the orange groves, and the women in muslin dresses standing in front of the cottages, and the river boats with their two smoke-stacks as tall as factory-chimneys, and the fruit vendors in crowded shops, and the beautiful white women and the beautiful mulattos and the negroes who have so beautifully developed figures. I have been making so many plans that I would need ten lives were I to fulfill them all. But in six weeks I shall give them up without sorrow and return, never to leave my home again. My eyesight has improved. I have been working, though very little. The light has been impossible, I have often been disturbed. My models are very kind, though a little too familiar, they do not take you very seriously because you are either their nephew or cousin. (Perhaps, if I find the time, I may bring with me a small, raw thing, but only for myself, for my room.) One cannot paint (*faire de l'art*) the same way in Paris and in Louisiana, it would revert into 'Monde Illustré' (into journalism). Indeed, it would require a long stay to acquaint oneself with the character of this race: by that I mean its charm. Such a brief period is a photography and nothing more.' The result of Degas' stay in America is pointed out in a letter from New Orleans to H. Rouart (dated December 5, 1872): 'Well, I undertook a journey and that is about all. Manet would see many prettier things here than I. However, he wouldn't be able to get any more out of it than I. We devote our art only to such persons or things as we have become accustomed to.' The result this time was a repetition of his visit to Italy: no deep impressions whatsoever. When he returned, Paris made a deeper impression than any previous experience. It was then that he got into contact with a group of young modern painters, and together they exhibited their works.

Degas went back to Italy several times. In 1873 he was there to see his dying father in Turin, at other times he visited his relatives in Naples. To complete the itinerary of his travels, though they were only temporary changes of scene, he visited Holland, Belgium and England and in 1889 he spent three weeks travelling from Spain, through Madrid and Sevilla, to Morocco and on to Tangier. This is what he wrote from Madrid: 'There is nothing, really nothing that would be able to give you an idea of Velasquez.' And from Tangier he wrote: 'In nature we love the kind of people who weren't unworthy to have touched it. I am saying this because Delacroix passed through this country.' But there were no sensations, no experiences that left deep impressions. Another quotation from Tangier: 'I have nothing to say, I am writing to you only to prove my friendship to you from Tangier. In about eight days I shall be in the *Rue de Chaillot*.' During the summer of 1888 till 1891, Degas stayed in Cauterets, a spa in the Pyrénées, where he underwent medical treatment, and with his friend Bartholomé, a sculptor, at the end of September and during October, he journeyed about Bourgogne in a tilbury, a kind of gig, drawn by a white horse. Bartholomé drove the carriage. The white horse was the subject of Degas' jokes as we can see from letters he addressed during the trip to his friends Halévy and Rouart: 'September 30, 1890. Bartholomé noticed that in the stable our white horse took the standpoint of a robust rascal towards your noble servant [towards Degas]. During our departure the horse made a cross and aggressive face at him, but afterwards, a kind of loneliness as well, as a look at the long and straight line of the road calmed the horse down. The animal feigned exhaustion in the town because he didn't want to leave it.' On October 1, 1890, Degas wrote from Melun: 'Our white horse is eating oats. In half an hour he will take us to Montereau. Everything depends on him, I really can't think about anything else. If the horse gets tired, we must be tired, too.' Montbard, October 14th: 'A horse's trot is much sweeter for a traveller than the gait of a woman . . . The horse has never been so well fed. He hasn't lost any weight, on the contrary, he is getting fat. Actually, I am willing to bet that no one would deny that the horse knows he is returning to Paris, he seems to know the direction without looking at the map.' Degas spent the years 1890—1893 in Switzerland. From Interlaken, one of the prettiest places in the world, on August 31, 1893 he wrote to Halévy: 'I can't live far away from my studio, I am unable to work. In a few days I shall be content.' His home called him.

Degas' life was not a pompous one. He never suffered from want. In the last decades of his life he sought more solitude, associating only with some old friends. He was growing blind. Already in the autumn of 1890 he complained about his eyesight in a letter to his friend, E. B.

Valernes, a painter: 'I can hardly read the newspapers. If in the morning, after coming to the studio, I am stupid enough to start deciphering them, I am then unable to work any more.' This is what Denis Rouart, the son of his friend tells about the last days of Degas: 'Almost complete blindness, the death of a number of friends, the war, the end of which he did not live to see, and—like the proverbial last drop which made the cup of sorrows overflow—the notice he was given to leave his studio, which was delivered to the mercy of the pickaxe, climaxed Degas' ill luck. He used to be seen wandering through the streets of Paris without an aim, and time and time again he would return to the site where his studio used to stand, the studio which had contained his whole life.'([6]) Edgar Degas died in Paris during the war, on September 26, 1917, at the age of eighty-three.

III With the Impressionists

The struggle for impressionism began in 1874. Degas was one of its chief instigators, although energetic behaviour and a capability to organise anything did not correspond to his character; and although he was never an impressionist—a fact which I hope to prove in this chapter. Not because impressionism represented a yoke which one ought to take off Degas' shoulders, but because it is important to use the right terms in their right places.

In Paris, on the *Boulevard des Capucines* 35, on April 15, 1874, in the former studio of a photographer, balloonist and designer by the name of Felix Tournachon Nadar, an exhibition was held. The group of artists who exhibited there called themselves *Société anonyme des artistes peintres, sculpteurs et graveurs*. Its founders were eight painters, Claude Monet, Camille Pissarro, Alfred Sisley, Auguste Renoir, Armand Guillaumin, Edgar Degas, Berthe Morisot and Paul Cézanne. These names represent a brilliant epoch in French painting, an epoch of immense importance for the development of art in all European nations. While reading the names of these eight painters, we can visualise their work and see that they did not share the same viewpoint on the conception of art. In the year 1874, it was the question of recognition that was in the foreground. Their works were eliminated from the official exhibitions or were represented there very insignificantly. And they were no longer young: Pissarro, for example, was already forty-four by then. Degas was forty, Cézanne and Sisley thirty-five, and Monet was a year younger. Their objective was to gain recognition. They invited other artists, thirty various painters exhibited 165 works. A critic by the name of Léon de Lora reviewed the exhibition in the magazine *Gaulois* under the following heading, *Exposition libre des peintres impressionistes*. And immediately afterwards in the paper *Charivari*, Louis Leroy's article bore the title: *Exposition des impressionistes*—perhaps because among the paintings Claude Monet's sunset was entitled 'An Impression'. This name, the impressionists, became very popular and for a short period was even accepted by the artists themselves; that is what they called their third exhibition in 1877 and during the time the exhibition lasted they published four numbers of a magazine *L'impressioniste. Journal d'Art*. But the fourth exhibition in 1879, upon Degas' request, had a different title, *Exposition des Artistes Indépendents*. This is what Caillebotte, a painter, wrote to Claude Monet about this change, 'Please, be kind enough to take part in the funeral procession and also be present at the actual funeral of the impressionist gentlemen for they have decided to call themselves "the Independents", because they discovered that the word "impressionists" meant nothing.' Between the years 1874—1886 there were eight of these exhibitions; the number of the exhibiting artists varied. Pissarro took part in all of them, Monet in five, Cézanne in two, Paul Gauguin exhibited his works at the fifth and eighth. Edouard Manet did not take part in any of these exhibitions though he was invited to do so. Degas exhibited his works seven times.

Degas paintings have nothing in common either with the technique or with the method of impressionism in the strictest sense. Degas did not break up colours, he did not apply paint on his canvas in small dabs of the brush, he did not apply the pasty thickness of paint; he did not sacrifice tone, colour, space or matter to the phenomenon of light and atmosphere; he did not paint only light and air like Monet, Sisley and Pissarro (at a certain stage of their complicated evolution); he did not impair either form or line by taking light into consideration. Degas, as the pupil of Ingres that he was, respected line to the best of his own belief and free choice; he did not rid shape or colour of cohesion; he worked like a constructor with precision when concerned with the problem of movement or when the question of composition was involved. He did not paint in the open air (en plein air) which was one of the principles of impressionistic methods, there are only a very few landscapes by Degas, dating back to his early youth, and a number of pastels and drawings which were done outside the walls of his studio in subsequent years. He had no intention of painting light, but people, horses, figures firmly placed into firmly limited space, or figures forming and filling up that space. Reality offered him not only impressions, but also experiences and very rich material for artistic reflections. He neither painted nor drew a momentary impression nor an instantaneous luminary state he might have experienced. On the contrary! All that has been mentioned here shows, I feel, that Degas was not an impressionist. Impressionism was, primarily, a matter of sight, and Degas' art, on the other hand, was more a matter of touch. Although literature claims that impressionism cannot be confined to such a strict extent, that an impressionistic picture plainly depicts an ephemeral impression, a transient or momentary movement, that an impressionistic picture indelibly intercepts an accidental fraction of reality — either way, none of these forms the substantial basis of an impressionistic painting.

Impressionism is comprehended in a still broader sense by Gustave Geffroy, who, typically, begins the first sentence of his work *Histoire de l'impressionisme* with the word *le soleil* — the sun. 'If I had wanted to restrict this study to only a special group (of impressionists), to a definite formula (of impressionism), I would have been able to mention only the paintings of Monet, Pissarro, Renoir, Berthe Morisot and Sisley. But I preferred not to divide those who were at one time a homogeneous group, whatever their later differences happened to be as far as their visions and ideals were concerned. This is a history of one moment, of one phase, not a history of a certain technique. These people struggled and were victorious together. That is why I have extended the formula of impressionism and mention in close parallel those who were primarily attracted by the phenomena of light, as well as those who were primarily attracted by social observations. If Monet set out on a passionate exploration of the cosmos of light, then Degas concentrated all the strength of his intellect on the physiology of forms and certain spectacles of civilisation.'[7] Geffroy's broad conception of impressionism does not coincide with the conception from the point of view of the fine arts. Impressionism does not mean an epoch, it is only an outstanding trait of that epoch, it is the apple of discord between the public and the artists as well as between the artists themselves. It is a very distinctly formed style of painting. 'Degas did not become an impressionist,' even Geffroy admits that, neither did Edouard Manet become one, and as for Cézanne, he wanted impressionism to become something reliable, respectable, solid and permanent, like art exhibited in museums.

Degas struggled, together with the impressionists, for the freedom of artistic expression, 'they are shooting us, but at the same time, they are turning our pockets inside out'. But he did not follow the same path. He said, 'The mistake of the impressionists consists in their effort to portray the air which is outdoors, which we breath; in short *plein air*. But the air seen on the pictures of great masters is not the air that can be inhaled.' Degas characterised the difference between the impressionists and himself in the following words, 'They need a natural life, I need an artificial one.' What then was this peculiar painter, this misanthrope who loved people, this impressionist who was not an impressionist? Is there one single expression that would characterise his art? Yes—and it is very simple even though we do read that he was one of the most complicated artists of his time.

IV Art

Before this word is written, the word that will very simply express the sense and contents of Degas' art, it is necessary at least to make an effort to reveal its complexity. I am not concerned with the problem of completely uncovering this complexity, neither do I intend to expound its entire contents. However, having been granted this opportunity, I feel it is my duty and obligation to give Degas' art some thoughtful consideration. Therefore I do not hesitate to draw the reader's attention to such questions that especially attracted me, as I followed from a distance the path Degas took, and as I read about it. I also thought it right not to suppress my desire to contribute a few words in defence of Degas' art. Meier-Graefe wrote that Degas was the most complicated artist of his time. In an effort to solve this complexity he began to tackle the problem by naming Ingres, 'For a long period of time, Ingres is what remained within the artistic being of Degas.' And in time, whatever else was imprinted on Degas' artistic consciousness, Ingres' academism lasted, with varying intensity, as its underlying tone. Degas loved Ingres and admired his painting immensely. Facing Ingres' portrait in the Louvre, he said, 'He was a man not to be trifled with!' But Ingres would say to his pupils, 'Nothing essential can be found in the fine arts after Pheidias and Raphael; it is necessary to copy them unceasingly to preserve the cult of truth and the tradition of beauty.' The mature Degas did not share this conception, because he preferred reality to Pheidias and Raphael, for he saw truth and beauty in it. 'While Ingres defines poses only, Degas was concerned with movements, and captured them.' Ingres' paintings lack the vitality of reality, the reality is transformed into a formula, it is deprived of individuality. In Degas' paintings reality is represented, it is stressed powerfully and is quite individual. The great Ingres stands for academy, antique culture, Raphael, conception. Degas stands for reality, nature, mankind, truth, experience. Degas possessed in his scrupulously chosen collection— which he passionately kept watch over and to which he constantly kept adding new works—

twenty pictures, thirty-five drawings and four prints by Ingres (by Jacques Louis David he had only one, a not very large study painted with raddle). The most numerous was his collection of Delacroix, thirteen paintings, twenty-four water-colours, thirty-six drawings, three pastels and twenty-eight prints. Sometimes, Delacroix's art is spoken of in connection with Degas' art, as far as movements of figures are concerned — 'the ability to secure the synthesis of movements' — and also when the optical combination of colours is apparent, and when the beauty of colours is concerned. 'For Jephthah' red garment keep in mind the orange-red tones of the old man in Delacroix's picture "The Taking of Constantinople by the Crusaders".' That is a note jotted down by Degas when he was painting the picture 'Jephthah's Daughter' (approximately 1860—1863). Far more important and veracious was the influence of Manet, who was primarily responsible for Degas' awakening to a realisation of the meaning of contemporary life. 'Degas was painting Semiramis when I was painting Modern Paris,' Manet would say and he was right. However, their relationship certainly went much deeper than that and also concerned matters of a technical nature in the art of painting.

Degas' first period which includes the days of his studies, his lengthy sojourn in Italy (1856—60), and the years in Paris immediately following, is commonly called his Ingresian era. Portraits constitute a majority of his work at that time. However, besides Ingres' influence, these portraits also show traces of Degas' studies in the galleries, traces of his work as a copyist, and at times, for example in the portrait of his brother, Achille de Gas in uniform of a naval cadet, painted about 1857, we are inclined to believe that he may have been influenced by what he had learned from the Italian portraits of the Renaissance. (I have in mind the portrait by Agnolo Bronzino.) But elsewhere, for example in the family portrait of the Bellellis and their two daughters, dated about 1860—62, there is already a certain newness which is quite obvious: it is an original Degasian conception. In his paintings depicting historical themes done in the first few years of the 1860's, there is, besides Poussin's impulse, a noticable trace of the severe, renouncing art of Puvis de Chavannes. 'No one else except Puvis de Chavannes was able to find such an absolutely right placement of figures in a composition. Try to move any one of his figures only a line or a dot and you won't succeed, it's quite impossible,' said Degas.

Degas' second period begins at about the middle of the sixties. At that time, the thematical contents of Degas' works underwent a change because of Manet's intervening influence. From then on, Degas belongs to his time and to the city that he loved so much. At the beginning of the seventies, Japanese woodcuts made an impression on Degas. In his collection there were woodcuts by Utamaro, Hiroshige, Hokusai and others. Meier-Graefe aptly expressed the degree and character of the influence that Japanese art had on Degas, 'It is inconceivable to mention the matured Degas without the Japanese contribution. It is just as evident in his work as the impulses received through Manet, and it was all to his advantage. It corresponded to his talent for drawing, it stretched the Ingresian line, actually changed, so it seems, a pupil of Ingres into a modern artist. This experience was of an inner quality. Degas never even approached the banalities of fashionable Japanese painting. An ethnographical motif of another race never worked its way into his paintings (as it did in the case of his friend Whistler). Degas treated Japan like Manet Spain. He kept himself at a distance. He was not a transgressive imitator, but an observer for whom the study of foreign countries was like studying nature, where he could gain experience; he gained everything that was valid. The Japanese style in his pictures is a typical segment (today, in motion picture scenarios, the word used is *detail*). But this segment seems quite European to us—it expresses completely our feelings. Everything we see, everything we experience is 'cut out' in this sense. Our senses require this form of perception. We want our dramas to have the same impulsive, unintentional style, truthful to the very last detail, so that the idea makes an impression upon us as if it were everybody's elementary emotion. However, this scope of Degas' pictures, (a classical example is the picture '*Place de la Concorde*' with Mr Lepic and his two daughters), this variety of movement and poses, this freedom of movement in the space of the picture, is not derived only from the Japanese example. From the beginning it is evident that the composition of the picture was one of the greatest, but never quite solved problems of Degas' meditations and efforts. He was a constructor, he always felt his figures in space, they were its part, they filled it out. This set him apart from the impressionists. He was a reflective composer of his pictures. 'If impressionism neglected the composition, then Degas is absolutely consumed by the word composition . . . His composition is not geometric but three-dimensional; his paintings are constructed with only one intention: to achieve the greatest possible depth on an area as small as possible.' (F.X. Šalda) [9] Degas studied very intensively in the Louvre, and there is no reason to doubt that his studies were mainly centred on the composition of a picture. It is my personal opinion that he learned or could have learned very much from the works from the 16th and 17th centuries. Some of Degas' pictures are composed from a variety of angles, working from the centre outward in different directions. This concerns the pictures 'Intermission' (1874) and 'The Washerwomen' (1879), the pastels 'The Ballerina' (1879), 'Conversation' (1880), 'Ballet Dancers Getting Ready for a Performance', etc. A composition of that kind, a composition developed from the centre, can be seen for example in the 'Cripples' by Pieter Brueghel Sr, a picture that Degas certainly knew very well from the Louvre because it is a unique work for a painter who is contemplating the composition of pictures and the conception of their space. In some other pictures by Degas, space is bent into the corner of a wall which typically slants sideways into space. This is obvious in 'The Dancing Class' (1874), 'The Office of the Cotton Factory in New Orleans' (1873), 'Absinthe' (1876), 'Ballet Rehearsal' (1879) and in many other pictures. Degas was able to study compositions of this sort from the paintings of the Dutch Baroque masters from the 17th century as well as from the Venetian pictures of the 16th century. Also the manner in which the figures are split in two by the frame of the picture, the 'occasional section', can be explained as a consequence of the Baroque composition. I should like to recapitulate that there is a balance on the scales of Degas' composition between the Japanese influence on one side and that of contemporary Europe on the other side, that Degas fully deserves the title 'typical European among modernists', given to him by Meier Graefe.

The new form of composition of Degas' pictures is also associated with contemporary photography. Degas himself photographed. There is a photograph of three persons in the studio, dated 1894 ('Degas in a very unaffected pose. Mme. Albine Fontane and myself. Degas composed this little group and Guillaume Lerolle took this picture at his signal,' writes Paul Poujard); the group is arranged in the fashion of Degas' 'matrimonial scenes' of the seventies. On several occasions, Gustave Coquiot [10], in his monograph on Degas, stresses the relationship between Degas' pictures and contemporary photographs. Germain Bazin [11], in reply, states that in Degas' time, photographers learned from painters and acquired their composition. It is right, indeed, but the relationship between the art of painting and the art of photography was more complicated. There are some photographs of the Paris street, dated about the year 1860, which in a certain sense anticipate the synthesis of painters. ([12]) However, the relationship between motives cannot be a criterion, because there still remains a great difference between a photograph, which represents an occasional section of reality, and a picture by Degas ('Place de la Concorde'; scenes from horse-races or from the ballet room) where reality is submitted to an organising will and the constructive idea of the artist. The will of Degas was firm and his constructive idea evident.

'Any art is less spontaneous than mine,' Degas used to say. (A photograph is spontaneous.) 'My pictures are a result of mathematical calculations as well as of an unlimited number of studies.' F. X. Šalda speaks of Degas' intellect almost as if it were a mathematical factor, 'Degas' intellect works like an infallible scientific instrument, there is not a single line left to accidental chance, mood or inspiration. Nevertheless, the final outcome usually looks innocent as if its creator followed an empirical method without regard to science and theory—so perfect is the removal of all the scaffoldings, so thoroughly is all the preparatory process removed, though there is no doubt that this process was very complicated and fatiguing.' Michelangelo's highest creative requirement is fulfilled: 'With the greatest zeal and employing one's best efforts and knowledge to try to complete a work that has involved the greatest of efforts, to make it seem as if it had been created quickly, without any efforts and with the greatest of ease.' Erudition and directness. Knowledge, and yet enchantment. All these definitions remove quite unjustly and forcibly his sensuality, his sense for beauty, as he understood it, and his sensitivity into the background of the creative process. 'Manet was a hot-tempered character, Degas was a rational character'—but we could in a certain sense invert Graber's definition. Getting into the colourfulness of Degas' oils, pastels and drawings, we find ourselves quite unmistakably in a field of the sensory enjoyment which arises from tasting beauty. We are in the artificial light of Degas' paintings. In the colourful haze there is something of the many-coloured lyricism of butterflies' wings, and of the refined words of poets, though otherwise Degas had nothing in common with their expressions. And yet, J. Huysmans, who first discovered Degas' importance and appreciated the newness of his art, wrote in a study about the exhibition of 'The Independents' in the year 1880, 'A painter of the modern era is born.' Edmond Goncourt ([13]) noted in his diary on February 13, 1874, after visiting Degas: 'For me he is a man who has, in his presentation of modern life, best expressed its soul.'

V Paris

Edgar Degas, 'a typical European among the modernists', by origin a not purely Frenchman, was the most pure-blooded and the most devoted Parisian. In this sense he was the heir of Honoré Daumier. In his collection, beside one picture and four drawings by Daumier, Degas also owned 329 of Daumier's lithographs and 416 folios of *Caricature* and *Charivari*. There is something exciting in the relationship between the names of these two men who are both among the greatest of artists. Baudelaire, who was one of the first to comprehend Daumier, wrote that he knew only two painters in Paris who painted as well as the beloved Delacroix — and that they were Ingres and Daumier. Michalet called Daumier a visualising philosopher who was able to express with one single picture more than one hundred articles in the newspapers; Daumier was the chronicler of the Paris people. To speak about Daumier is to speak about Paris of his time. Daumier's art is a grand show of his time, where there are no actors, but life itself plays the leading part. Degas, who belongs to the next generation — twenty-six years separated them — was more particular. He chose only certain waves from the human ocean of Paris. Daumier was a general practitioner for everybody — Degas was a specialist. Daumier really wanted to cure — for he fought against human triviality, meanness, stupidity, brutality, he wanted to educate. Degas did not cure, he registered with precision, as if he had used a microscope. Degas' friend, Forain, once said, speaking on behalf of all the caricaturists of his and of the previous epoch when Daumier was being compared, 'Oh, Daumier, he is quite apart from us. Daumier was magnanimous.'

Daumier showed Degas the way into some thematic spheres; Degas became his follower for example in the whole theatrical sphere, in folk entertainments, in the theme of the washerwoman. However, Daumier's washerwoman is marked by the hardships of life, Degas' ironer is perspiring and yawning. Daumier, in the sense of Romanticism of his days, and in conformity with his human aims, had a regard for the human soul, he mentioned it even in places where he found it painfully lacking. Degas had in mind, first of all, the activities of human beings, their movements, the basic laws of movements, yet he did not lack the emotional foundation. There is a great number of Daumier's themes which Degas did not follow. But he did discover new ones in the face of Paris.

He discovered the world of horse-races, the millinery and laundry shops and the world of the ballet studio. Degas exchanged Daumier's country-fair stalls of the jesters for a world of cabarets. In front of a street-stall of troupers on the outskirts of Paris, one is likely to hear the hollow sound of a drum — that is Daumier. In Degas' ballet studios one can hear the soft strains of a violin. Degas' art is more intimate. A woman, a naked Parisian girl in countless poses, Degas-the-painter's greatest love, does not exist in Daumier's work at all. Let us not forget that even that period spoke to them in different voices, that they belonged to two different generations, that there was no longer anything romantic in the thoughts and imaginations of Degas. Let us also not forget that Stendhal's description of life and woman's love is different from that of Maupassant.

George Moore narrates about Degas' cafés: *Café Guerbois, Café Nouvelle Athènes*, where Edouard Manet and Edgar Degas used to preside over the society of artists, each at his own table. Among those who used to meet there were Renoir, Pissarro, Monet and Sisley. After Manet's death, Degas used to visit the *Café de la Rouchefoucauld* . . . Moore characterised Degas by saying that there was nothing striking either about the way he dressed or about his behaviour. But for those who knew him he was typical in his greyish suit and blue necktie fastened around a loose collar. George Moore continues his account by mentioning that those who knew him intimately say that Degas' rounded shoulders, waddling gait, his clear, hearty and articulate masculine voice were features which personified him. Anyone who happened to visit the café would have had to have been gifted with an above average critical mind to discover that Degas was no ordinary person. He blended with his surroundings. Gustave Coquiot follows Degas through the streets of his quarter; he passes by the windows of ironing shops and laundries; he drops in at the shops of milliners, the theatres on Montmartre, the circus Fernando which Degas made famous through his painting of an acrobat called Miss Lola; he continues on by naming the cabarets and *cafés-concerts* that Degas used to visit and that were fashionable in his time; he recalls the names of the singers and the titles of their popular songs; he lists the names of well-known race-courses—Longchamp, Chantilly, Vincennes—'It was a heroic era for horse-racing in France, which lasted from 1872 to the end of the century.' Coquiot goes on to name the tram and omnibus routes that Degas took, lists all the routes of those vessels which sailed the Parisian ocean from whose platforms Degas used to inhale the life of Paris, whose safe platforms Degas would flee to, as if they were floating islands of his happiness.

From the mid-sixties it was Paris that gave Degas' art its contents. In 1866 Degas' first painting with the race-course theme appeared in the Salon. The picture of musicians in the orchestra was painted about 1868. 'Woman Ironing' was painted in 1869, and in 1872 Degas painted his classical masterpiece, 'The Ballet Scene from the Opera Robert the Devil'; and it was also the year he did his pictures from the ballet studios. At the first exhibition of the Independents in 1874, Degas' entire thematical programme was almost completely developed: a ballet rehearsal in the theatre, a scene in the wings, 'Woman Ironing', 'The Start of the Horse-races', 'After the Bath'. At the second exhibition (1876), new themes were added: 'The Milliners', 'In the Café'. At the third exhibition, (1877), 'A Dancer on Stage', 'A Singer at a Café-concert', 'Woman Bathing', 'The Ballet'—completes the catalogue of the themes. The Parisian woman was the dominating motif.

'Degas became a miraculous interpreter of the manners of his days, of the clothing, of certain gestures, of parts of the face of that period. Degas observed with penetrating eyes, he was able to portray whatever he saw with matter-of-factness, dignity and ingenuity. When looking at Degas' pictures, we see a part of the world through his eyes. He gave us certain formulas for the phenomena of life which are as factual as the articles of our daily use, like certain quickly spoken words in common conversation. Nevertheless, he remains foreign to us, like one of those countless, nameless heads of industry who produce the things necessary for our daily use and which we are so used to that they are no longer able to excite our fantasy.' The meaning of these penetrating sentences voiced by Meier-Graefe is that the art of Degas is, let us finally utter this simple word which expresses its nature, realistic.

'*Il faut être de son temps.*'
('*One must be subject to his own time.*')
(H. Daumier)

VI The Realist

As a painter, as a draughtsman, as a sculptor, Edgar Degas was a realist. He was a realist in the sense that he was concerned with the conception of nature in men and things. His work gave us a great deal of pure scientific description of the human body, of the soul and of the milieu of his time, of his town. He was a realist as are only a few artists of our present or past days. He is a realist like Brueghel, like Rembrandt, like Goya. He is a realist of the sort who does not form reality for himself alone, but who, by painting reality, gives of his own intellect, his feelings, his love for the body and manifestations of life, and who, above all, keenly observes reality without succumbing to mere appearances or impressions. He was more realistic than Gustave Courbet, he knew nothing about allegory, and was closer to the current day, he was not a bohemian. He was like Millet—but Millet bestowed his own charming sweetness upon his peasants, whereas Degas was truthful. He was a painter of truth.

How did he intend to seize reality? In his sketches he made a draft of his working procedures on how to learn to know the world. He drew in series. 'A series of musical instruments in their various shapes; the various gestures of musicians, the bending of their arms, the twists and turns of the shoulders and necks of violinists, the puffed-up and normal cheeks of the wind instrument musicians. Innumerable evening motifs. The various *valeurs* of plastic shapes reflected in the mirrors of *cafés*, many details; the arms or legs or hips of the ballerinas. Draw their dancing slippers; the hands of a hairdresser; bare legs in dancing movements. Proceed simply: for example, to draw a motionless profile while moving about, changing my own position; applying this same method when drawing the entire body; the same for numerous movements of arms and legs while dancing—they remain where they are but you walk around them. Make studies of human figures or of things from various angles of perspective, it is possible to use a revolving mirror; you do not have to change your position, only the mirror would revolve or be slanted toward or away from the objects.'

This sounds rather like a treatise about painting from the early period of the 16th century. There are further series, series of things that are alive. 'All sorts of paraphernalia that would reflect the life of the person they belonged to; it might be a corset that has just been taken off, which for a certain brief moment will retain the shape of the body.—A series of aquatints about sorrow. Various blacks; a black veil covering the face, black gloves, hearses resembling Venetian gondolas. A series of various palenesses of a face. A series of smokes, smoke from pipes, cigars, cigarettes, from locomotives, from factory chimneys, from steamers, smoke that is bent while a steamer is passing under a bridge. A series of a baker's utensils. Bread. Baker's apprentices in the cellar, perhaps seen through a cellar window from the street. Pink flour. A still-life of slices of bread in perspective abbreviations. Carefully assorted baker's products, tarts, grain, small mills, flour, sacks.' This is the huge supply on stock belonging to the artist-realist. The method of the painter-realist is his awareness of the reality of shapes, things, people, movements. The extensive detailed knowledge—as far as the nude woman is concerned—was mastered by Degas to a degree of perfection. While admiring Degas' works, you need not think of virtues, of heroism, of sacrifices, you can remain on earth and say to yourself: fashion, hat, soap, bathtub, powder, make-up, comb, and you will love these things which did not fall from heaven.

'A painter of modern life!' says one Czech critic, 'Degas is an actual classic of modernism, he sees modernness in a monumental fashion, stylishly; he synthesises and enchants it into a new convention which will deliver the character of this period to future generations. A philosopher of the future will be able to discover the character of our time from the brutal arabesque into which Degas inserted modern bodies—in case all other documents are lost.'

Degas says, 'To draw a piece of nature and to master that same piece of nature into a composition, are two diametrically different things.' Degas' realistic art is complicated. Within its realm there is 'discipline, instead of inspiration, which is a vulgar gift of too many a painter . . .' (F. X. Šalda). Another definition states that Degas' art is a unity of inspiration and reflection. As a painter he was a learned man. He used to say, 'Art is not at all a device of entertainment and amusement. Art is renouncement.'

George Moore, speaking about Degas, mentions that he once bought a drawing of a woman's hand by Ingres and looked upon the details of the finger nails, the way they were outlined, with extreme admiration. Finally, Degas pointed out that Ingres' drawing was what he considered to be the work of a genius: Ingres considered the illustration of a hand to be so seducing, so charming and so difficult that he became reserved, all his life content that he did not know how to do anything else but sketch and draw finger nails.

Degas' realism is not of an encyclopaedic quality, it is not an illustration for an atlas on anatomy, it is neither photographic nor professional in volume. What a blasphemy for Coquiot to say that Degas' horses are draft horses to be hitched to some sort of vehicle, and that his jockeys are cabbies who weigh at least eighty kilogrammes. He is blaspheming art. For Degas' pictures of the race tracks are not concerned with thoroughbreds nor with the jockey's weight. Meier-Graefe, as if in answer to such calumny, says, 'Degas' pictures always have, though they be disputable, an anatomic matter-of-factness bordering with encumberance.' And here is a quotation concerning Degas' horses: 'Degas' horse has nothing in common with the stallion of the Gros School, it is not the sympathising fellow-sufferer, fellow-rejoicer of Delacroix's heroes, whose horses' eyes sparkle and nostrils quiver with excitement. Degas' horses have breeding. I am convinced that they are horses bearing a certain excellence of that time. The tapster would probably know their names even today.'

Degas' realism is passionate, fierce and never satiable. The ballerinas, the ballet dancing studio, the stage, the backstage . . . Gauguin wrote about Degas' dancers, saying that they are not women. 'They are machines at work that have charming lines and a balance that verges on the miraculous. They are products like hats from the Rue de la Paix, including all their delightful artificiality.' Degas himself used to say that his ballet dancers were only a pretext to be able to draw. This is a point we cannot but disagree with. He painted and drew the ballet dancers on stage, during their strenuous rehearsals, while they were relaxing or tired and weary. He drew them because they attracted him as a painter by their gestures, movements, by their filmy, butterfly-like costumes, by the symphony of the white or glitteringly exquisite colour of their skirts and bodices in the footlights, they captivated him as a piece of life in which he lived and which he loved so passionately. Not even the hats from the Rue de la Paix did he paint like the delightful knick-knacks that they were, but rather like vanity and joy, like an ornament and an indispensable part of a woman, like temporariness passing through the restlessness of time. Degas' art was in correlation with life, it was derived from life, it was an expression of life. He would capture the ballerinas in the different poses and figures of their dance, thus creating, unawared, a manual, a sort of living book of patterns or a kind of film of the classical ballet—just like Goya who, in his Tauromachy, created a manual of the noble art of toreadors. Degas' pastels and drawings of ballet dancers became, in the course of time, simpler and simpler, while the outlines as well as their effects became more monumental and so, in the end, they turned into a kind of symbol or prototype of the motif they represented. This symbol, prototype, substance, this idea of the phenomenon, of movement, of the sign of life—is the lasting, lawful, unimpressionistic, durable and permanent element in Degas' work. It does not anaesthetise, it does not paralyse. Degas' realism is movement itself. Straightening out their low-necked costumes before the performance, the arms of the ballerinas move like a wind-driven wheel of a mill, and the arms and legs of the seated ballet dancers while relaxing are composed into an ornament like a rosette. They are not machines, they are women. It is not an artificial or fictitious mechanism; it is a tedious profession and a painfully acquired art. Degas' realism is a realism of emotions. In his pastels, pictures and drawings, Degas very deeply, carefully, nobly and with human understanding described the psychology of a prima ballerina who experiences her outstanding performance on the stage, her glorious moment.

Degas' realism is a realism of the senses. Since the woman drying and combing herself after a bath, as Degas used to portray her with undiminished sensory excitement again and again, is neither a mathematical problem nor a geometrical instrument. Degas' pictures and drawings of nude women do not show an expression of a cool mathematician and sophist, but ingenuity and passion obviously have participated in the result. His pictures and drawings join the qualities of the perfect composer of fine arts and a man who is infinitely curious and who is infinitely surprised by the beauty of womanhood. For Degas' nudes are a part of nude life; and life is neither a measure nor mathematics. This fact is not in discord with what Degas claims: that he would like to paint a woman without her knowledge, that best of all he would like to gaze at her through a key-hole.

VII The Drawing

Degas used to say, 'One can become a painter, but one must be born able to draw. I was born a draughtsman. I am a colourist of lines. Working in colour means developing on the depth of a drawing.'

No matter how enchanted we may be by the colours of Degas' oils and pastels, the essence of the art of Degas the painter is drawing. Ingres used to say to his pupils, 'Drawing is the honest substance of art. By drawing I do not mean only tracing the contours. A drawing itself does not depend only on a line. A drawing is also an expression, an inner form, a plan, modelling.' Ingres' pupil, Degas, enlarging upon his teacher's instructions (which he mastered perfectly) adds the following: 'A drawing alone is not a form, it is an experience of a form, or it is the means of seeing a form. It accents the form and pattern.' Degas' drawing is not ornamental, it is not calligraphical, it is not pretty; its beauty is in its veracity. And it is alive. One of Degas' friends, a critic and a realistic writer, Edmond Duranty devoted a few words to contemporary drawings in a booklet called 'New Forms of Painting' (which he published in the year 1876 on the occasion of the second exhibition of the *Société anonyme des artistes* which took place in the Durand-Ruel gallery), keeping in mind, above all, the drawings by Degas. These are his words, 'Today, we do not strive to attain calligraphic lines or contours, decorative elegance of lines, nor do we aim to copy grecian form of the Renaissance. A drawing of today wants to acquaint itself thoroughly with Nature and achieve as close a union with her as possible. The aim is—as far as form is concerned—to be faultless and to know an infinite variety of types. Let us do away with the tendency to handle the human body as if it were a vase, its decorative roundness being the important aspect. Down with the unchanging monotony of the frame of the body and down with the bulging muscles under the skin! We need a special distinctive feature for the fully clad modern man amidst the human bustle, at home, in the streets; it should be a study of the mental reflections in his face as well as in his clothing. We do not want to see lines measured with compasses but forms that are alive and bold; forms that have logically developed from within. This drawing [Degas'] is so individualistic and is such a personal means of expression that we cannot try to derive any method, process or opinion from it. It intimately unites with the aim and it is an unseparable companion to the idea.' In other words, Degas' drawing is not what was learnt, it does not characterise the beginning of the painter's pilgrimage, but it is a constant aim of this journey; it does not follow any preceding form or opinion, it has no scruples which might rise from any known schemes, it is not stylish in any sense of the meaning of this word and, of course, it is not naturalistic. It is not a hook whereon to hang various expressions or ideas; indeed, Degas' drawing itself is the expression and the body of an idea: of dance, virtuosity, fatigue, display, intimacy; it is the expression and the body of life and character. George Moore wrote that Degas draws the character. The method, aim and contents of Degas' drawing is truthfulness. Had he been teaching a group of pupils in a house several stories high, this would have been his method; on the uppermost floors they would have started by copying the drawings and etchings of the old masters. On the third floor their lessons in painting would continue by studying and using as models the exquisite works of the great old schools. On the second floor they would have had a try at their own compositions and in this way they would come closer to the live models on the first floor; they would not have worked with this kind of model before, not until they had had several years of training first. What, fundamentally, does this mean? That it is not wise to begin with reality and then to withdraw from it, no matter how you choose to go about it, but, on the contrary, one should always come nearer to reality, always keeping it in mind as the aim, coping with it again and again, not understanding reality as a means, but as an end. One should not practise on reality, but appear in front of reality fully equipped and ready in the technical and human sense.

'All his life Degas probed as much in the sphere of aesthetics as in the sphere of a painter's technique.' Denis Rouart, in his study concerning Degas' technique ([15]), goes through the whole list of his various accomplishments. Towards the latter part of the 1880's, Degas was abandoning all other painting methods except for pastel, of which he became a matchless master, and which best suited his need of experimenting. 'At first, around the year 1880, he tried to blend pastel with tempera; later on, he sprayed the unfinished pastel with water and then he continued to work with a brush. He expressed himself more and more by using a wider surface and richer range of colours. He used conspicuously visible dashed lines without trying to blend or unite them, to obtain stronger contrasts or harmonies of colours and tones, through the use of contrasting or related colours. After having accomplished some experiments with calking pastels in 1892, until the end of his life he continued, unceasingly, to strengthen this tendency towards attaining ultimate perfection. The colours became more brilliant, the brush gained a greater width and strength, the accents became more distinctive and the contrasts more expressive. In accordance with this development of technique, the conception of composition also changed by becoming simpler and more harmonious. The range of vision was reduced and included only a limited area (not as before, for example, the entire large ballet studio), where only a few bending figures could be placed who covered each other up and who were severed either by the frame or otherwise.'([16]) This is evident in Degas' pastels and drawings of nude women and ballerinas whose arms, legs, trunks and heads form admirable ornaments of composition, their most exuberant liveliness being in perfect balance with the principal laws of painting.

In his youth, Degas the draughtsman was captured by Ingres' technique. He drew with a sharply pointed lead; with precision, with clean-cut lines. During the period when he began to turn away from Ingres' influence, he also changed his painting tools. He used soft pencil whose black line was more expressive on paper. (Rouart uses the word *pierre noire, pierre d'Italie*.) He took a fancy to charcoal, owing to the lively, thick, easy to shape, variously shaded, and colourful lines it made; in the end, it was his only drawing tool. He used charcoal (similarly to the way he used pastels) for his studies when calking, drawing on tracing paper. This method suited his passion which was a constant search to capture movement at its most forceful point, to give his composition the most constricted and at the same time the most effective shape and expression, and to give his pastel the most beautiful combination of colours. 'With Degas, a drawing took first place. It really became a religion for him, an obsession, he was almost possessed by it. Throughout his whole life, he served this passion only.' (Rouart). In the year 1892, Daniel Halévy made a note of a conversation his grandmother had with Degas:

Degas—that outstanding man of reason: 'Reason! You are speaking about reason? What is it? Nothing can cause more stupidities than reason. Don't use it except for getting into a bus.' Mrs. Halévy: 'But what if tomorrow, someone were to say when speaking about you that you had lost your ability to reason? Would you like that?'

Degas: 'Well, it would not keep me from making a good drawing!'

Some of Degas' drawings were studies and the bases for his sculptures. Degas began to model in wax in the middle of the sixties. At first he made studies of horses in motion. In 1880 or 1881 he made a wax figure of a fourteen-year-old ballerina in a linen bodice and a tulle skirt —the figure is very touching and pathetic in her simple, humanly unaffected beauty. Rewald's catalogue ([17]) makes a note of fifty-three sculptures made between 1882—1911; these are for the most part nude dancing ballerinas. Ambroise Vollard once met Auguste Renoir on a boulevard. They stopped in front of the Opera at Carpeaux's statue, called 'The Dance', and they began to talk about it. Renoir cursed it. He said, 'Why, the dance that is performed in the Opera has a tradition, has a certain aura of sublimity, it's not a cancan . . . And moreover, we are fortunate enough to have a sculptor who is able to compete with the old ones.' Vollard opposed, 'But Rodin was commissioned to make the statue of "The Philosopher", Victor Hugo, and "The Gates of Hell".' Whereupon Renoir retorted, 'Well, but am I speaking about Rodin? I said: the first sculptor! And that is Degas.'

In a letter dated January 20, 1903, Paul Gauguin wrote to his friend de Monfreid, 'Degas is said to be rude and sarcastic. But that does not hold true of those who, in Degas' opinion, deserve his attention and respect. He has an instinctive heart and mind. As far as his talent and behaviour is concerned he is a rare example. He is what every artist ought to be. He was admired by members of the exclusive clique, Bonnat, Puvis, Antoin Proust etc., and never wanted any favours from them! He was never heard to have used a rude or uncouth word or have said anything ugly in any sense. And nothing of that sort was ever said about him. Art and dignity!'

Degas, nature and art, reality and order, heart and reason, passion and sentiment, temporality and eternity, balance, beauty and truth.

List of Plates

1. *Old Beggar in Rome*, black pencil, drawn on light green paper; 420×270 mm., signed: Roma, 1856.
   In 1856, Degas left for Italy where he stayed a number of years. He worked there under the influence of Ingres, whom he had previously studied. It was not only the environment of Italy, but his devotion to Ingres' artistic manner as well, that influenced the drawing of the beggar, whose face has a tragic expression. Like Delacroix in Tangier, Degas found old Romans in Italy. Agamemnon lamenting for Iphigenia, who was to be sacrificed.

2. *Portrait of a Young Woman Wearing a Bonnet*, lead pencil; 290×220 mm., about 1860—1861.
   The influence of Ingres' drawings is evident. However, even in this fine, tender drawing, Degas' analysing and penetrating style of art can be seen.

3. *Portrait of the Painter J.J. Tissot*, charcoal; 310×350 mm., about 1861.
   If the date of this drawing is marked correctly, it visibly contradicts the historical themes Degas painted during that period, about 1861, because there is a certain degree of unaffected spontaneity in this drawing. Its whole conception is quite real and apt for that time.

4. *Study of Two Clothed Figures*, lead pencil; 328×215 mm., about 1864.
   A drawing from Degas' series of historical paintings, possibly for the painting 'Jephthah's Daughter'. Reminiscences of his stay in Italy and a certain amount of pathos in form are clearly visible. However, these characteristics shortly vanish from the painter's work.

5. *Standing Nude*, a study for the painting 'Disaster of the City of Orleans', lead pencil; 355×218 mm., 1865.
   A drawing based on reality, reminiscent of Ingres' drawings, but this influence is almost suppressed due to Degas' increasing critical feeling for reality.

6. *Study of an Archer* for the painting 'Disaster of the City of Orleans', charcoal and ruddle; 223×343 mm., 1863.

7. *Portrait of Mrs. Hertel*, lead pencil; 357×232 mm., signed and dated 1865.
   The drawing clearly presents contemporary features. It is a woman belonging to her time.

8. *Study for the portrait of E. Manet*, lead pencil on pink paper, 413×280 mm., about 1864—1866.
   Study for an etching. It shows fine workmanship, almost tender, also the characteristics of the features and face are gently and attentively portrayed.

9. *Study of Rider on Horseback*, essence on ochre paper; 250×340 mm., about 1866—1867, Paris, Louvre.
   From 1866, Degas belongs to his time.

10. *At the Race Tracks*, essence on ochre paper; 450×310 mm., about 1865—1867, Paris, Louvre.

11. *Young Jockey*, lead pencil; 285×230 mm., about 1866—1868.

12. *Study of an Arm of a Woman* who is on the right side of the picture 'Miss Fiocre in the Ballet "La Source", 'charcoal and pastel 310×230 mm., possibly 1868.
    The drawing is economical; its tender realism is emphasised and transposed to a higher realm due to the artist's sensual attraction.

13. *Portrait of Mrs. Camus at the Piano*, charcoal; 350×220 mm., about 1869—1870.
    The intimity of the room. Luminary effects. Degas' twilight tones.

14. *Study of a Woman* for the picture 'Two Women Dressed in City Clothes Repeating a Duet',

lead pencil on coarse paper; 480 ×300 mm., about 1868—1870, Paris, Louvre.

15. *Study of a Woman* for the picture 'Two Women Dressed in City Clothes Repeating a Duet', lead pencil on coarse paper; 480 ×300 mm., about 1868—1870, Paris, Louvre.
Both studies change Ingres' lifeless lines into unaffected, spontaneous, lively lines. They were preparatory sketches to an unfinished painting—one of those in which Degas approached the modern works of contemporary literature.

16. *Seated Ballerina with a Hand on Her Nape*, essence on dark blue paper; 210 ×260 mm., 1874. Study for the picture 'Rehearsing Ballet on Stage', an exceptionally lively draft of visual perception.

17. *Standing Ballerina with a Raised Left Hand*, charcoal and chalk on pink paper; 450 ×280 mm., 1874.
Study for the picture 'Rehearsing Ballet on Stage'. Artificial light, luminary reflexes.

18. *Standing Ballerina with Arms Behind Her Head*, India ink and gouache on green paper; 538 ×445 mm., 1874.
Study for the picture 'Rehearsing Ballet on Stage'.

19. *Standing Ballerina with Hands Behind Her*, charcoal and chalk on brownish-grey paper; 450 ×300 mm., 1874.

20. *Standing Ballerina Fastening Her Belt*, India ink and gouache on coarse paper; signed; 545 ×375 mm., about 1874.

21. *Two Standing Ballerinas*, one from the back, the other in profile. India ink and gouache on brownish paper, 300 ×310 mm., about 1874—1875.

22. *Two Studies of a Ballerina* from the back, black pencil and chalk on pink paper; 455 ×310 mm., about 1874—1875; a study for the picture 'Ballet Studio'.

23. *Study of a Head and a Sketch of Bending Ballerina*, charcoal and pastel on pink paper; 460 ×300 mm., about 1874—75.
A drawing showing great emotion and delightful movements.

24. *Ballerina Scratching Her Back*, black pencil on greyish-pink paper; 440 ×294 mm., about 1874—75, Paris, Louvre.
Study for the picture 'Ballet Studio'. Painter was delighted by shiny hair and by an involuntary movement of hand.

25. *Standing Man with Hat, Leaning on an Umbrella*, oil on brown paper; 330 ×200 mm., about 1875 .This drawing is very timely in type and in clothing.

26. *Undressing Woman*, oil on brownish paper transposed on canvas; 610 ×500 mm., about 1875.
Probably first idea for figure of woman on the picture '*Le viol*'.

27. *Bowing Ballerina*, black pencil and chalk on grey paper; 440 ×300 mm., about 1875.

28. *Ballet Master*, essence on ochre-green paper; 475 ×300 mm., signed and dated 1875.
Study for the picture 'Ballet Studio', which is in the Louvre.

29. *Two Ballerinas Leaning on a Bar*, essence on pink paper; 220 ×270 mm., about 1872—75.

30. *Three Women in City Clothes*, black pencil, charcoal and pastel; 440 ×630 mm., about 1875—76. Signed.
Note in pencil, '*Portraits en trise pour décoration dans un appartement*'.

31. *Standing Ballerina*, in profile, black pencil on pink paper; 475 ×370 mm., about 1875—76.
Unbeautified reality; opposite of academism.

32. *Woman with a Parasol*, essence on canvas; 750 ×850 mm., about 1875—76.

33. *Ballerina Bending Forward*, charcoal and chalk; 340 ×290 mm., about 1875—76.
34. *Ballerina Adjusting Her Ballet Slipper*, essence on pink paper; 380 ×310 mm., about 1875—78.
35. *Ballerina at a Bar*, black pencil; 305 ×194 mm., 1877, Paris, Louvre.
36. *Ballerinas at a Bar*, essence on green paper; 465 ×610 mm., 1877, signed.
37. *Two Resting Ballerinas*, charcoal and chalk; 300 ×460 mm., about 1876—80.
38. *Mélina Darde*, black pencil, 305 ×230 mm., signed and dated: December, 1878.
39. *Miss Lola from the Fernando Circus*, charcoal and pastel on coarse paper; 470 ×320 mm., January 25, 1879.
   Study for the painting exhibited at the fourth exhibition of the Impressionists in Paris, 1879.
40. *Portrait of Etcher Martelli*, charcoal and chalk on brownish-red paper; 420 ×300 mm.
41. *Three Sketches of a Young Nude Ballerina*, charcoal and chalk on greyish-green paper; 480 ×630 mm., about 1876—80.
   Study for wax sculpture 'Fourteen-year-old Ballerina', which was exhibited at the 6th exhibition of the Impressionists in Paris in April, 1881.
42. *Four Sketches of a Young Ballerina*, charcoal; 480 ×300 mm., about 1876—80, Paris, Louvre.
   Study for wax sculpture 'Fourteen-year-old Ballerina'.
43. *Seated Ballerina Putting on Tricot Shirt*, black pencil; 320 ×225 mm., about 1878—80.
44. *Standing Ballerina*, in profile, pastel on ochre paper; 600 ×450 mm., about 1878—80.
45. *Singer from Café-concert*, charcoal on grey paper; 465 ×300 mm., about 1878—80, Paris, Louvre.
   Study for a painting and for a pastel.
46. *Two Studies of a Singer from Café-concert*, charcoal and pastel on grey paper; 575 ×445 mm., about 1878—80. Signed.
47. *Woman Adjusting Ribbon on Her Hat*, charcoal and pastel; 480 ×310 mm., about 1878—82, Paris, Louvre.
   Study for the pastel 'At the Milliner's'.
48. *Standing Ballerina Raising Right Leg*, charcoal and chalk on greyish-green paper; 465 ×610 mm., about 1879—82.
49. *After Bath*, essence on canvas, 1510 ×2150 mm., about 1880—82. Sketch for an unrealised painting.
50. *Woman Washing Herself*, charcoal and pastel; 620 ×470 mm., about 1883.
51. *Ballerina Standing on One Foot with Right Arm Raised*, pastel on ochre paper; 225 ×305 mm., about 1882—85.
52. *Three Ballerinas*, charcoal and pastel on grey paper; 450 ×595 mm., about 1885—88; signed.
53. *After Bath*, woman drying herself, charcoal on tracing paper (calk); 410 ×280 mm., about 1885—90.
54. *Nude Woman Combing Herself*, pastel; 425 ×280 mm., about 1889—90, signed.
55. *Bath*, charcoal on tracing paper.
   Drawings Nos. 55—60 are variations of a motif Degas did in the 1890's with charcoal on tracing paper, in order to be able to change and study it again and again. It was as if he kept rediscovering the artistic interest of this motive as well as its human attractiveness.
56. *After Bath*, charcoal on tracing paper.
57. *Bath*, pastel on tracing paper.
58. *Bathing Woman*, charcoal on tracing paper.

59. *Woman Drying Herself*, charcoal on tracing paper.
60. *Woman Combing Herself*, charcoal on tracing paper.
61. *Bathing Under Trees*, charcoal on canvas; 1620 × 1930 mm., about 1894.
62. *Two Ballerinas*, charcoal, 500 × 390 mm., about 1892—95.
    Study for Columbine and Harlequin.
63. *Two Washer-women*, charcoal on tracing paper; 570 × 420 mm., about 1892—95, signed.
64. *Woman Leaving a Bath*, charcoal on tracing paper; 543 × 255 mm., about 1899—1902.

Notes

(1) J. Meier-Graefe, *Degas*, Munich, 1920. (A book of basic significance for studying Degas' art.)

(2) Ambroise Vollard, *Degas*, German edition, published by B. Cassirer, Berlin, 1925.

(3) Ludovic Halévy, in co-operation with Meilhac, wrote comedies as well as libretti of Offenbach's ope-rettas. Degas presumably took part in staging their comedy, 'La Cigale', in 1834.

(4) *Les lettres de Degas*, edited by Marcel Guérin. Daniel Halévy is the author of the preface. New edition, published by Ed. B. Grasset, Paris, 1945.

(5) J. Meier-Graefe, *Degas*.

(6) Denis Rouart, *Degas*, Graun & Cie., Paris, 1949.

(7) Gustave Geffroy, *La vie artistique III. Histoire de l'impressionisme*, E. Dentu, Paris 1894.

(8) Roger Marx, *Degas*, *L'image*, 1897. (Free Trends, Volné směry, No. XI, 1907.)

(9) F. X. Šalda. *Impressionism: Its Development, Results, and Successors*, (Progressive Revue, Pokroková revue), No. V, 1907—1908. (Reprinted in *Sanctuary of Sight*, Hájemství zraku, by F. X. Šalda, Melantrich, Prague, 1940.)

(10) Gustave Coquiot, *Degas*, Ollendorff s. a., Paris.

(11) Germain Bazin, *Degas et l'objectif*, L'amour de l'art, Vol. XII, 1931.

(12) *Un siècle d'élégance francaise*, edited by Chène, Paris, 1943.

(13) Excerpt from Goncourt's diary is reprinted in H. Graber's book *Edgar Degas nach eigenen und fremden Zeugnissen*, Schwabe, Basel, 1942. (Second edition.)

(14) Ernest Rouart, *Degas*, *1937*.

(15) Denis Rouart, *Degas à la recherche de sa technique*, Floury, Paris, 1945.

(16) Denis Rouart, *Degas. Collection: Palettes*, Braun, Paris. 1949.

(17) John Rewald, *Degas, Works in Sculpture*. A complete catalogue, Pantheon Books, New York, 1944.

Bibliography

Coquiot Gustave, *Degas*, Librairie Ollendorff, Paris, 1924, second edition.

Faure Elie, *Histoire de l'art.*

Fosca François, *Degas*, *Les albums d'art druet*. VI. Paris, Librairie de France, 1927.

Geffroy Gustave, *La vie artistique. Troisième série. Histoire de l'impressionisme*, E. Dentu, Paris, 1894.

Graber Hans, *Edgar Degas nach eigenen und fremden Zeugnissen*, B. Schwabe, Basel, 1942, second edition.

Guérin Marcel, *Les Lettres de Degas*, Edition B. Grasset, Paris, 1945.

Henri Hertz, *Degas. Art et esthétique*, Librairie Félix Alcan, Paris, 1920.

Ingres raconté par lui même et par ses amis, Vésenaz - Genève, P. Caillen, 1947.

Meier-Graefe Julius, *Degas. Ein Beitrag zur Entwicklungsgeschichte der modernen Malerei, Piper & Co., Munich, 1924*

Moore George, *Modern Painting.*

Moore George, *Confessions of a Young Man*, William Heinemann, London, 1917.

Munther Richard, *Ein Jahrhundert französischer Malerei*, S. Fischer, Berlin, 1901.

Rewald John, *Degas, Works in Sculpture*, Pantheon Books, New York, 1944.

Rouart Denis, *Degas à la recherche de sa technique*, Floury, Paris, 1945.

Rouart Denis, *Degas. Collection: Palettes*, Braun et Cie., Paris, 1949.

Rouart Denis, *Degas dessins*, Braun et Cie., Paris, 1948.

Rouart Ernest, *Degas*, Paris, 1937.

Šalda F. X., *Impressionism: Its Development, Results, and Successors* (Impresionismus: jeho rozvoj, resultáty i dědicové), Progressive Revue (Pokroková revue), No. V, Prague, 1907—1908.

Šalda F. X., *Informative Introduction* (Informační slovo úvodem), Catalogue of the XXIIIrd exhibition of the society of artists 'Mánes': French Impressionists; Prague, 1907.

Vendrès Nicole, *Un siècle d'élégance française*, Les Editions du Chene, Paris, 1943.

Vollard Ambroise, *Degas, 'Artistes d'hier et d'aujourd'hui'*, G. Crès & Cie., Paris, 1924.

L'amour de l'art, Vol. XII; Number 7 is devoted to Degas; articles by Etienne Moreau Nelaton, *Deux heures avec Degas;* and *Degas et l'objectif* by Germain Bazin; Paris, 1931.

DRAWINGS

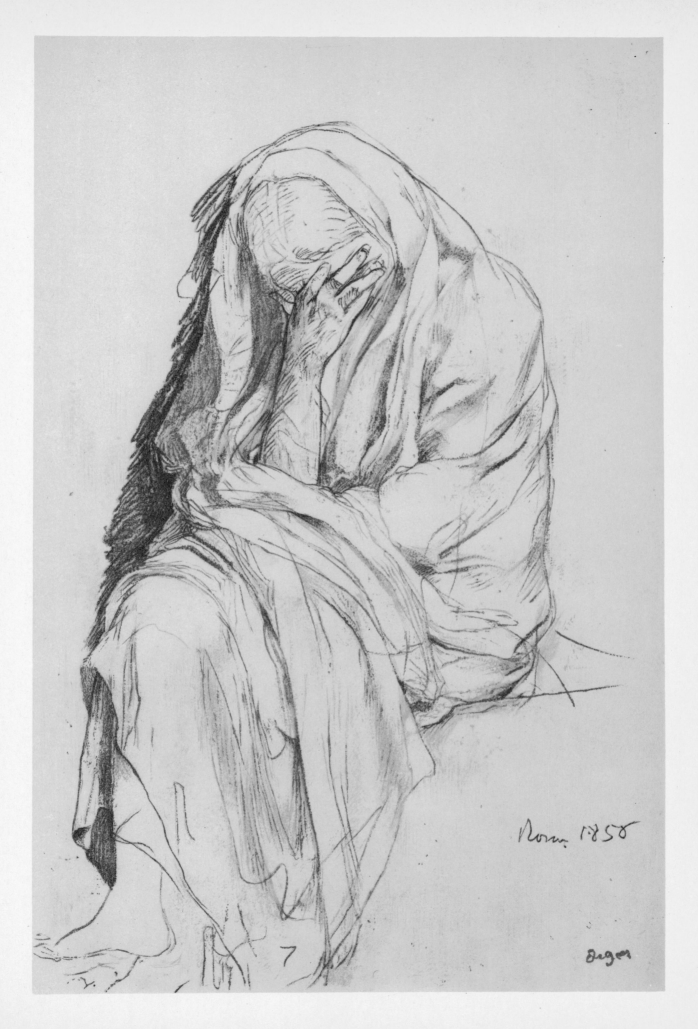

Rom 1858

Degas

I

Degas

4

5

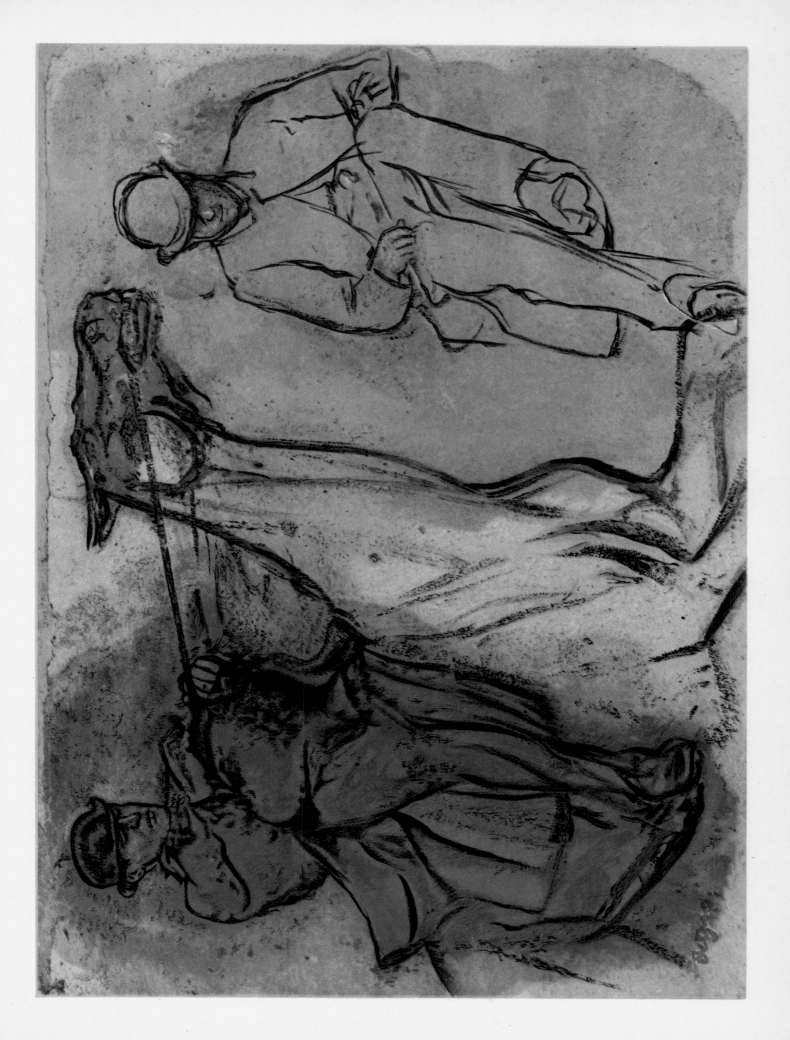

9

Degas

Degas

Degas

24

25

26

Degas

Degas
1875

28

33

36

37

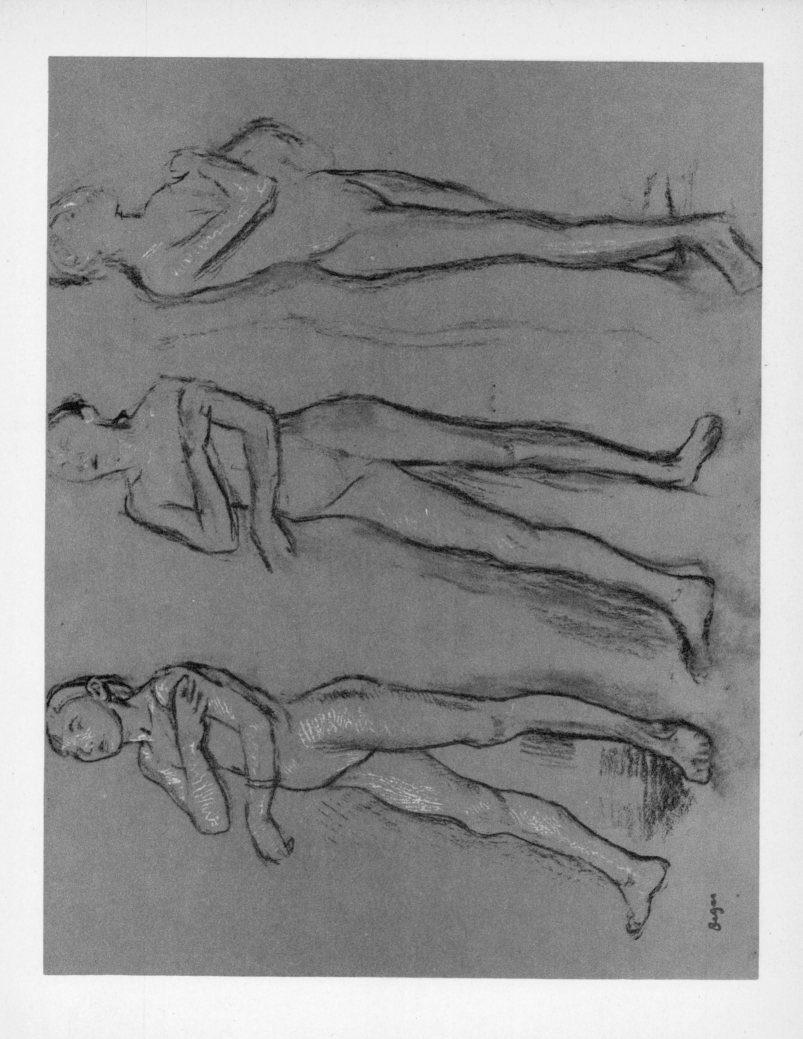

Degas

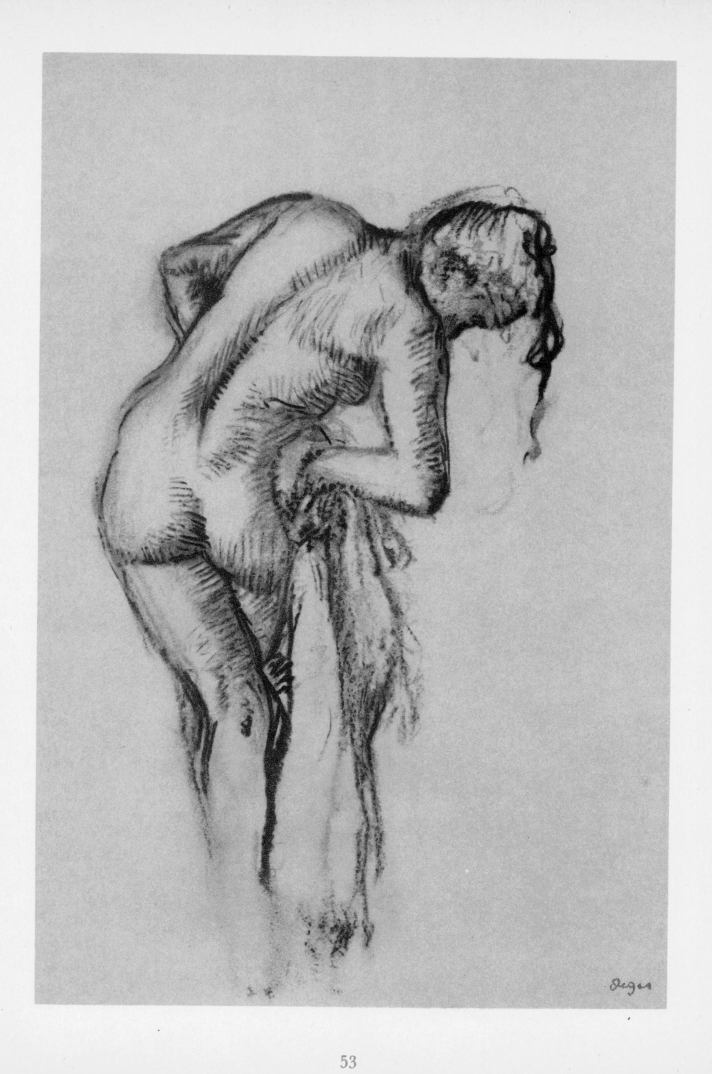

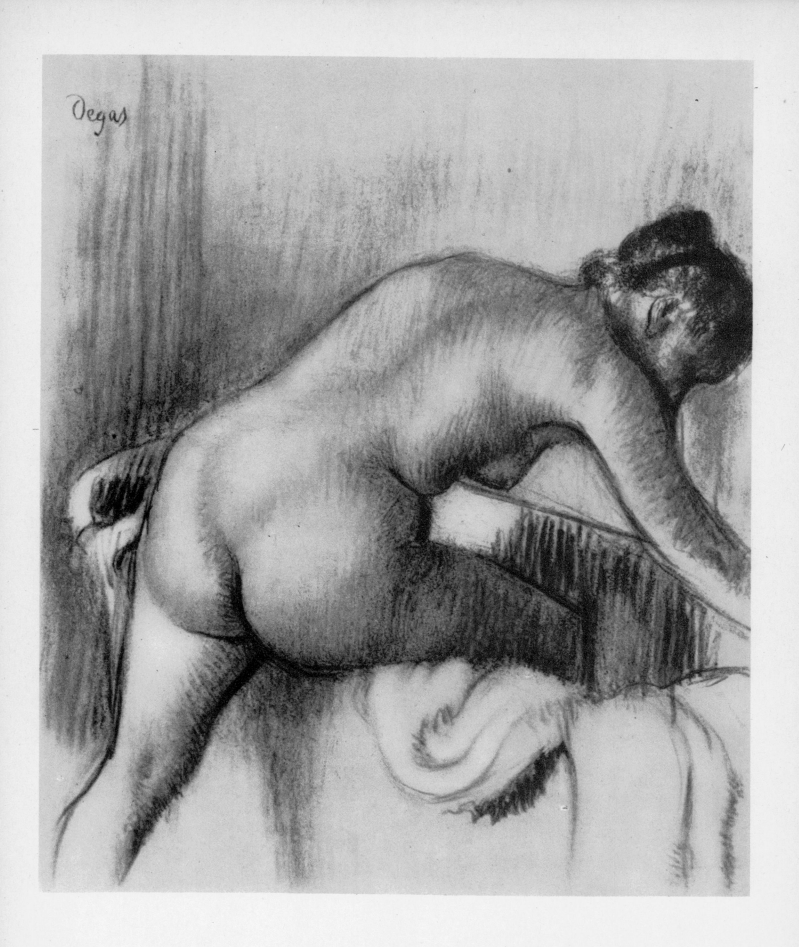

55

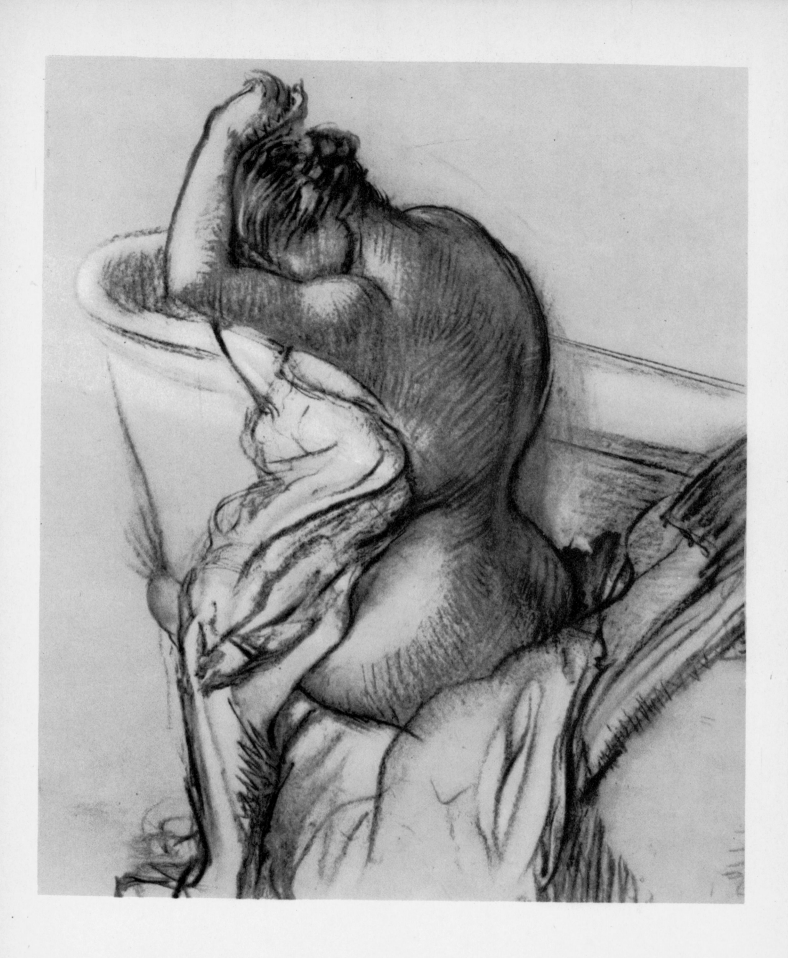

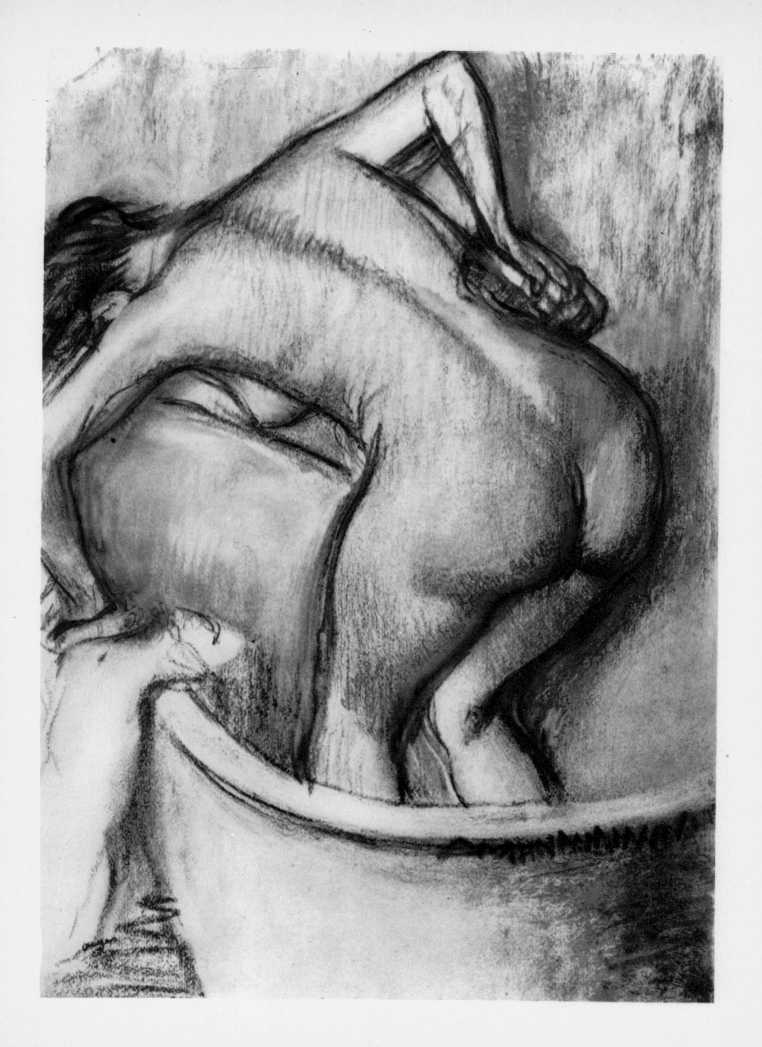

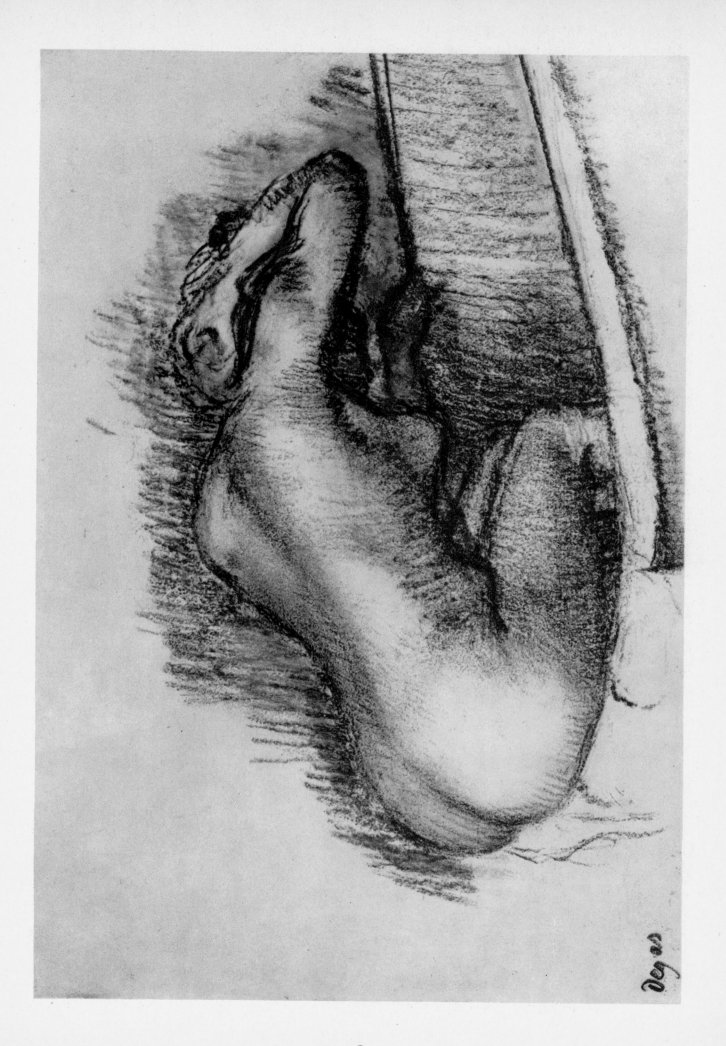

58

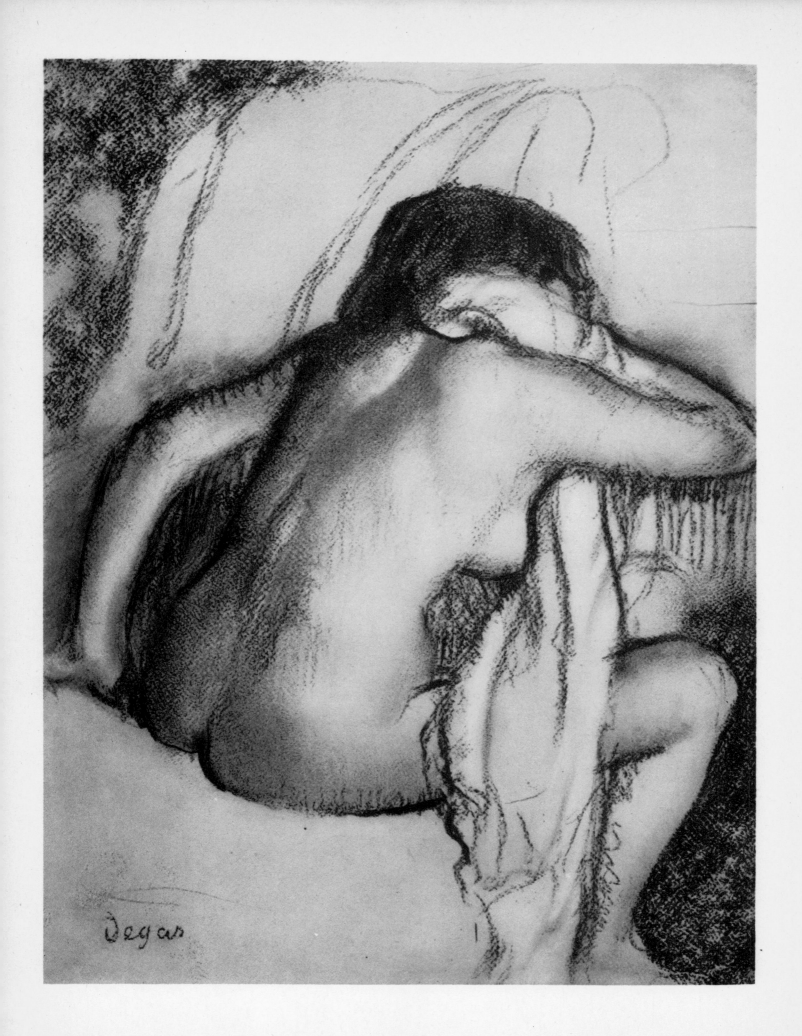

Degas

Degas